Architectural Expressions

Peter and Tony Mackertich

Archite

Expres

A Photographic Reassessment

ectural

sions

Fun in Architecture

Peter and Tony Mackertich

acknowledgements

The cameras used for the majority of photographs were Nikon F2 Photomic, Nikkormat EL, Nikon FE and Nikon FM, with a range of Nikon lenses. Films were exclusively Kodak, either Ektachrome professional transparency, or Kodachrome. For the more recent photography, the film has been Ektachrome VS. The photographs on pages 13 (below), 20 (below), 21 and 120–1 were taken on 120 film, and in these cases the camera used was a Hasselblad 500C/M or SWC.

Special thanks to:

Carol Cass	Maggie Toy
Claire Plimmer	Ian Colverson
Hamish Pringle	The Boss
Keren Weinstin	The Invictaworkers
Sari Finch	Mike at Technique
Pauline Nee	Tomasz Zaleski
Chris & Larence Curtis	Judy Martin
Abigail Grater	Our Mum and Dad

First published in Great Britain in 2001 by
WILEY-ACADEMY

A division of
JOHN WILEY & SONS
Baffins Lane
Chichester
West Sussex PO19 1UD

ISBN: 0-471-49667-7

Other Wiley Editorial offices
New York • Weinheim • Brisbane • Singapore • Toronto

Designed by Christian Küsters @ CHK Design

Printed and bound in Italy.

contents

introduction

"Less is more."
– Mies van der Rohe, 1947

"Less is a bore."
– Robert Venturi, 1969

"Less is only more when more is no good."
– Frank Lloyd Wright, *The Future of Architecture*, 1953

"The lower the culture the stronger the ornament. Ornament is something that has to be conquered."
– Adolf Loos, *Ornament Verbrechen*, 1908

Aside from their many other more usual pursuits, photographer and art director Peter and Tony Mackertich have spent the last 30 years wandering the world and collecting by way of photography images of architecture which inspired and motivated them. Peter Mackertich explains: "We took the pictures for the majority of these from, I'd say, about 1971/72 onwards. And it's been added to, and added to, so there's never been an exact idea of 'we've got to record all this'; it's just as we found things. During that period of time there were modern buildings appearing. There was never the same response to architecture of the 1960s and '70s. I've looked for decorative buildings of the sixties and seventies, and they're very difficult to find. They do turn up. There are some American buildings that fit that timetable, but not many. It was a particularly barren area for surface decoration. You wouldn't have found many architects actually wanting to put surface treatments on things."

This volume is a record of their work and a lesson in the joy that architecture can bring. The initial interest was a reaction to the buildings that were being designed en masse around them in the 1970s. Buildings that they found monumentally boring. Plain grey concrete walls, soon streaked with rain deposits, or small family homes that have one simple pattern and were repeated the world over. This was not a reaction in general to Modern buildings – or buildings of the 'International Style' – quite the contrary. The Royal Festival Hall on London's South Bank, for instance, is revered as one of the most wonderfully exciting buildings, full of clever design and a great deal of individualism. But the Mackertichs do feel – similarly to many – that whilst there were many great buildings being constructed, there was still a loss of a sense of fun within the built environment. Perhaps the earnest intentions of those who sought to recreate architecture for the populus actually alienated them as they lost the sense of enjoyment that the built environment can provoke. There is also a sense that sometimes certain design styles were being applied for use in the wrong buildings. As an example, the Hayward gallery on London's South Bank is criticised for having the appearance of a concrete bunker. Both the Mackertichs have a particular appreciation of the bunker as an object, but this is dependent on its situation. Peter has photographed bunkers across Europe, but to place such a building as a focal gallery in a capital city shows, they feel, a lack of understanding of the enjoyment and excitement public architecture should inspire.

Throughout the Modern Movement there was a desire to be true to materials, to banish ornament. This in itself was a reaction to over-ornamented Victoriana which began to represent an extravagant and overindulged society. A society which favoured the rich and left the poor behind. With the beginning of the new century and two world wars came the desire to represent a more egalitarian society, and the banishing of ostentatiously ornamented architecture was generally deemed as the most apt method. In the long term perhaps this can now been seen as ironic, but then it was a natural reaction to what had gone before. Architects no longer wished to apply surface decoration. It became seriously unfashionable to do so and it seems this was a part of an alienation between architects and the general public who, although perhaps unaware that the intentions were good, had a tendency to feel that their desires were not being considered. Tony Mackertich believes that architects did not see it as responsible to apply surface decoration: "It's not seen as architecturally credible, because you are being flippant in terms of the brief." There is of course the financial aspect: although a great deal of public perception can be driven by the architects, it is in the end the patrons who dictate where the money is spent. Surface decoration can be argued to be unnecessary – depending on how it is designed – and therefore is perhaps the first element to go on any economy drive!

Over the last three decades, however, architecture has moved into a pluralistic age whereby architects and building designers do not have an overall style that they feel obliged to follow. Whilst there is a still a hesitancy in many designers to be frivolous, there is a wider acceptance of styles and inspiration and so designers can follow much more their own inspirations and stimuli to create for the community what it is that they believe is wanted by that community. This is of course why we have such a wide range of architectural styles being executed across the world.

Architecture has always been a clearly serious pursuit created in order to enrich the lives of those who experience the buildings, but the Mackertichs feel that many architects became somewhat 'over earnest', perhaps losing the desire to give a sense of fun to their creations. It is all too often felt that the architects enter their work with a certain degree of arrogance, wanting to implant onto the horizon a creation which makes its mark as a monument to the designer. The Mackertichs both understand and disapprove of this action. If the building gives something back to the community, creates a sense of enjoyment and fun, then it is acceptable; but if it is merely stark, unyielding and monumental then this is not acceptable. The buildings presented here are a collection by two people who have experienced architecture across the world: the book is a personal album, but it does serve as an interesting lesson to us all!

Peter Mackertich: "But don't you think architects have always been led by the nose? They've always wanted to be able to tell us – the non-architects – 'This is the way it's going to look, and you should believe us, because we're professionals.' Certainly in the '50s and '60s architects stamped a distinctive look on buildings. They'd always believed that when they destroyed something like Euston railway station – the arch – what was going to be built there would be something of comparable standing. But what was built there was in actual fact a totally ordinary office block. They would say, 'Trust us; we know; we're professionals.' I think that's why we've ended up with such mediocre city centres. Liverpool, Leeds, Manchester, Birmingham ... we've been let down by what we've been given. We've been let down in the sense that what we've been given is second-division, post-Bauhaus thinking: concrete walls, very, very plain surface treatment, almost devoid of any kind of visual link with what was originally there."

To a certain degree many of these criticisms are entirely unjust. A great deal of consultation and research is carried out before and during the development of these schemes; they are not simply the dream of one sole architect. Peter Mackertich appreciates this element and in fact believes this can be part of the reason for the lack of success in some of these designs: "The more people involved (in the design process), the less radical the piece of work will be. I think that people do actually dilute it. The democratic process dilutes architecture." Tony Mackertich adds: "Interest in self-expression rarely occurs in architecture. I can't think of any buildings that have got real self-expression other than the ones that we like." Self-expression is a key reason for the selection."

Despite the dominance of certain styles in architecture, there were still many designers creating schemes that made people smile as they walked by and Peter and Tony have done their best to seek these out and to capture their beauty and fun. The theatrical drama of a building is what gives it the appeal. The reaction it provokes. Tony Mackertich describes how looking at Will Alsop's Peckham Library is an experience which lifts the spirits – it appeals and amuses. Future Systems' Lord's Media Centre, also in London, has a similar effect. Interestingly these two buildings have won the Stirling Prize for architecture in subsequent years. They are truly individual statements that stimulate a positive and possibly inquisitive reaction in the observer – at the same time, of course, as perfectly performing the function for which they were designed.

Whilst over the years the architectural profession has oscillated with its opinions of various types and styles of architecture – from "Less is More" (Mies van der Rohe, 1947) to "Less is a Bore" (Robert Venturi, 1969) – the general public is on the whole searching for enjoyment and pleasure in the built environment. Although of course the overriding desire is for perfectly functioning buildings.

One of the most intriguing aspects of this incredible collection of architectural curios is that alongside the buildings widely accepted as works of genius by architectural cognoscenti and lay people alike – Gehry's Guggenheim Museum in Bilbao, Alsop's Library in Peckham and Future Systems' Media Centre, Lord's, London – are placed the Tail o' the Pup hot dog stand, the LA donut sellers and the Aztec roadside Hotel. This vital characteristic of the collection makes it a unique tale, a true insight into the excitement of architecture, a perceptive grouping of imagery to question architects and to inspire all who wander through the journey on which the photographs take us.
Some buildings will be considered fashionable by the architectural community, whilst others are not so appreciated. But fashion is frequently a fickle animal.

Peter Mackertich: "Ultimately, I think that the real connection between them all is that they evoke a sense of good will, good humour, good vision. You get a good vibration from seeing them."

This book is put together to celebrate that invigorating quality and power that architecture can have, not only to function as shelter, but also to inspire those who encounter and experience it. *Maggie Toy*

... and in the beginning

Architecture was born at the moment when early man, making shelter for himself, first began to think beyond the mere practicalities of structure. Aesthetics came into the equation, and the act of building was instantly taken to a different level. But for millennia thereafter, architecture adhered to principles which, whilst in a constant state of development, tended to maintain a certain level of 'seriousness'.

Through the centuries, various rules of layout, proportion and symbolism produced buildings with an almost complete range of emotional impact: the awesome power of the ancients, the meditative serenity of the Romanesque, the soaring spirituality of the Gothic age, the homeliness of Arts & Crafts and vernacular architecture... But one trait was almost invariably missing. Until relatively recent times, buildings lacked a sense of humour and fun. The 19th century witnessed the occasional outburst of fancy and fantasy – the mad Prince Regent's Royal Pavilion in Brighton at the beginning of the century, and all the works of Antoni Gaudí in Spain at the end of it, come into this category – but mainstream architecture maintained its straight-faced sobriety. This chapter presents two notable structures which brought a new dimension to architecture, each breaking the mould in its own way.

The Michelin Building in London was built to house England's first purpose-built tyre-fitting garage, as well as head offices for the Michelin firm. It is representative of a certain type of late Victorian/Edwardian architecture that, rather than imposing an unrelated style with its own connotations, makes a feature of its product and celebrates it. The ornamentation on the building unashamedly incorporates various representations of rubber tyres – on their own and in piles which resemble the torso of the Michelin Man himself, who is featured in his entirety in a variety of poses. The façade is largely clad in ceramic, with painted tiles depicting motoring and aviation heroes, as well as purely decorative faience mouldings coated in brightly coloured glazes that add to its exuberance.

The Einstein Tower, on the other hand, does not feature a decorative scheme at all. Its appeal lies purely in its extraordinary organic form. It is a quieter vision than the fantastical confections of Gaudí, but is equally otherworldly. The structure was built to house a laboratory and observatory for Albert Einstein, whose theories revolutionised perceptions of time and space by enabling them to be viewed as fluid and malleable. Erich Mendelsohn reflected the great scientist's theories in his design by producing a building which itself appears to be malleable, containing not a single straight line. Refusing to be limited by his materials, he managed to produce the effect he desired using brick and concrete. This building has never ceased to inspire, and is as impressive today as when it was built over eighty years ago. *Abigail Grater*

Above: tyre and Michelin Tyre Company MTC motif

Michelin Building, 81 Fulham Road, London, England, 1911, by François Espinasse (photographed in 1975)

Opposite: ceramic visual exuberance to sell tyres

Right: tiles by Gilardoni Fils et Cie to designs by Ernest Montaut (Coupe Gordon-Bennett, 1904; driver: Théry; car: Richard-Brasier)

COUPE GORDON-BENNETT 1904   THÉRY sur RICHARD-BRASIER   PARIS

Michelin Building – tiles by Gilardoni Fils et Cie to designs by Ernest Montaut; Coppa Florio, Brescia, 1907; driver: Minoia; car: Isotta-Fraschini

"Architecture is the art
of how to waste space."

– Phillip Johnson, 1969

Michelin Building

Opposite: nunc est Bibendum!
(Bibendum in glass, 1985)

Above: detail of wheel with
rubber plant

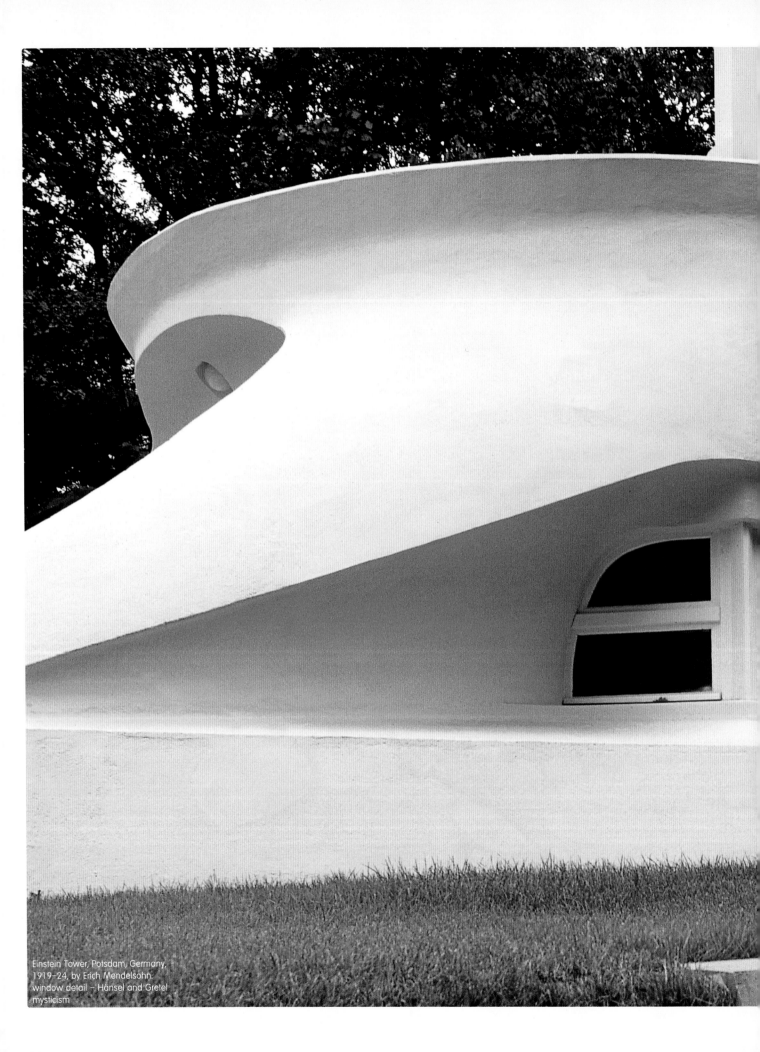

Einstein Tower, Potsdam, Germany, 1919–24, by Erich Mendelsohn: window detail – Hänsel and Gretel mysticism

Einstein Tower

Above: the expressionistic
stairway and entrance

Right: the astounding laboratory,
home to the
theories of modern physics

Opposite: the highly
esteemed tower

"I look at old buildings, at Erich Mendelsohn's Einstein Tower. I speculate that if Mendelsohn were still alive today he would have done all the things I've done and I would have had to go somewhere else."

– Frank O Gehry, quoted by Giles Worsley in *The Daily Telegraph,* 18 March 2000

ancient
visions
through a
windscreen

For centuries, architects have made direct references – both structural and ornamental – to the buildings of earlier times. Revivalist movements have been par for the course. On the whole, however, even these were carried out with an air of gravity. The interest tended to be largely antiquarian and involved the expounding of yet more theories – theories regarding the sources of the original forms, the symbolic significance of motifs, even the morality of the architecture itself.

With the discovery of Tutankhamen's tomb in 1922, Egyptomania burst onto the scene. This was a revival with a difference. Naturally, serious archaeological investigations were being made; but the proliferation of designs they sparked off was far from serious. Suddenly all manner of things were decorated with Egyptian motifs, with little or no regard for their appropriateness to the objects or structures they adorned. The concern was not to be 'correct', but simply to revel in the exuberant form and technicolour splendour of the ancient structures and artefacts. Soon Assyrian and Aztec designs were undergoing the same treatment.

This chapter presents six buildings which represent this new attitude to old form. Four of them were originally designed as factories – a building type which until recently had been considered too mundane to qualify for decorative treatment. These examples are endowed with ornamentation that is a pastiche of that on which it is based, with authentic motifs quoted in a humorous, almost sacrilegious way. The Samson Tire Factory is inspired by the palace of the Assyrian King Sargon II – which, like the factory, covered an area of 23 acres – and winged figures which were originally considered guardians of the grave are used simply to imply strength and fantasy. In the case of the Carreras factory, the sacred feline of the Egyptians is poached in a reference to the company's Black Cat cigarette brand, named after the cat that used to sit in the window of the original shop.

Positioned on major highways, these buildings – with the exception of the much later Homebase store, which follows in the same vein – are also among the first to have been influenced by the increasing ubiquity of the car, designed as they are to make an immediate impression on drivers in the brief moment they take to pass by. The factories in particular were intended to inspire the onlooker to admire the modernity of the companies in question by virtue of the ultra-fashionable Art Deco buildings they had commissioned. The decorative forms are entirely superficial, but the spirit is infectious. *Abigail Grater*

Carreras 'Black Cat' Factory, Mornington Crescent, London, England

Opposite: Mark Wadwah's retro redevelopment with Egyptian painted columns

Left: roof, window and cat detail

Below: full view of main façade

"Bauhaus with bells on."

– Simon Callow on the Carreras 'Black Cat' Factory

Firestone Tyre Factory, Brentford,
London, England, 1928, by Wallis,
Gilbert and Partners (demolished
1980) – gone but not forgotten

Firestone Tyre Factory

Opposite above: columns and lanterns flanking entrance from the A30 road

Opposite below: ceramic Firestone logo

Right: ceramic tiles around doorway

Below: bronze door in front entrance

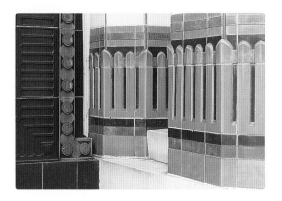

"I am for the art of bright blue factory columns and blinking biscuit signs."

– Claes Oldenburg, 1961

"To build a factory in the form of a temple is to lie and disfigure the landscape."

– Mies van der Rohe, 1920

Hoover Factory, Perivale, London, England, 1932, by Wallis, Gilbert and Partners (photographed in 1976, before it became a Tesco supermarket)

Opposite: decoration on entrance

Above: general view from the A40

Right: metal door detail

Samson Tire Factory, Telegraph
Road, Los Angeles, California, USA,
1929, by Morgan, Walls and
Clements

Below: view from Telegraph Road

Right: crenellated roof detail

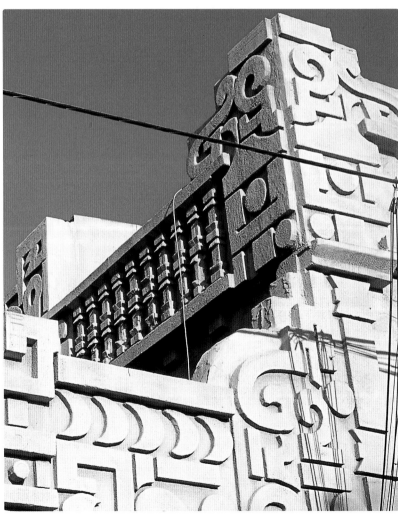

Above: Samson Tire Factory
bas-relief Assyrian warrior Herod
with a handbag!

Top, right and opposite: Aztec Hotel,
311 West Foothill Boulevard,
Monrovia, California, USA, 1925, by
Robert Stacy-Judd (still in use as a
hotel)

Homebase, Warwick Way, London,
England, by Ian Pollard, c.1986

Opposite: Egyptology comes to DIY

Above: Egyptian gods overlooking
the car park

ship-shape
and moderne

Following the craze on the ancients, architectural inspiration took a huge leap forward in time to focus on new technologies and, more specifically, the most fashionable modes of transport. In the USA in particular, the late 1920s and '30s saw a proliferation of buildings which incorporated sweeping, streamlined curves and stylised mechanical form.

One of the great icons of 20th-century architecture, the Chrysler Building is the archetypal New York skyscraper. Its brief stint as tallest building in the world was put to an end after only a few months when the Empire State Building was constructed; but despite being taken over in stature and prominence by many other subsequent structures, its magnificence and charm have never diminished. It is the ultimate Art Deco showpiece, with its decorative forms inspired by components of the motor cars manufactured by its commissioners, the Chrysler Corporation, in a bold commercial statement. Giant winged radiator caps take the place of gargoyles, and enormous sculptured hubcaps are transformed into a dazzling lantern which quite literally crowns the building.

The other buildings featured here derive their brand of Art Deco from the ocean liner, which was in its heyday at the time of their construction. They differ from the Chrysler Building in another important way: their formal references bear no relation to their purpose. As with the buildings in the previous chapter, the use of the new forms was simply a question of fashion and fun rather than appropriateness, and of achieving an air of the grandiose within a light-hearted, modern context. Some are near the ocean, others are entirely landlocked; some make open references to ship features such as portholes, funnels and walkways, others take on more abstracted forms combining sweeping lines with geometric elements. Colour adds a further dimension to the liveliness of these buildings, from the ice-cream pastels of the hotels to the crisp, clean red-and white of the Coca-Cola bottling plant.

Meanwhile, in Europe, the 'respectable' face of architecture was dominated by practical, minimal, geometrical Modernism, rather than the quirkier Moderne. The Bauhaus was undisputed king throughout the 1920s, into the '30s, and for several decades beyond, its influence spreading further afield in the later years. No self-respecting architect would dare turn his hand to designing a building with an overt sense of fun. *Abigail Grater*

Coca-Cola Bottling Plant, 1334 S
Central Avenue, Los Angeles,
California, USA, 1937, by Robert V
Derrah – landlocked in tarmac.

Coca-Cola Bottling Plant

Clockwise from left: gangway and porthole detail; the Big Bottle; section of ship; bridge detail

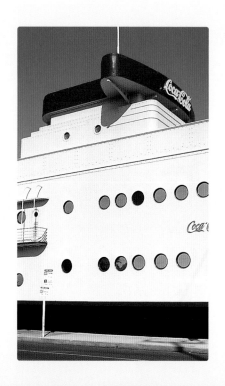

Opposite: Crossroads of the World, 6671 Sunset Boulevard, Los Angeles, California, USA, 1936, by Robert V Derrah

"Elvis has just left the building."

– Frank Zappa, 1988

Opposite top:
Crossroads of the World –
ship as shops

Opposite bottom:
Shelborne Hotel, Miami, Florida,
USA, 1954, by Igor B Polevitsky –
big type

Top:
The Greystone Hotel, Miami,
Florida, USA, 1939, by Henry
Hohauser – cassata architecture

Bottom:
Miami Hotel, Collins Avenue at
14th Street, Miami, Florida, USA –
suntrap moderne

Chrysler Building, Lexington Avenue
at 42nd Street, New York, New York,
USA, 1928–30, by William van Alen

Below: radiator and hubcap detail
over 42nd Street

Opposite: shimmering stainless
steel vertex

Chrysler Building

Opposite: mid levels with step backs

Left: entrance from Lexington Avenue

Above: the lantern, icon of Art Deco

wit in
wonderland

Divided into three sections, this chapter highlights some oases in the desert of humour during the period when the International Style reigned supreme. These are buildings that say – or, rather, shout – what they are. They are all about putting the subject matter of what's in the building on the outside of it.

The first section, 'Big Fun', features playful buildings in which the dictum 'form follows function' – coined by Louis Sullivan in 1896 and hijacked by proponents of Modernism – takes on an entirely new meaning. The structures express their function with their form, although here this is not merely a matter of the relationship between room function, plan and façade, but of the building taking on the shape of the things it is designed to produce or sell. An enormous hot dog houses a fast food seller; a drive-through doughnut entices drivers with a sweet tooth; a photography shop takes on the form of a huge camera. A music company headquarters resembles a stack of records, a tailoring factory features a bobbin-shaped cupola, and a house for space-age living rises above a hillside like a flying saucer. A few of the buildings here display playfulness for its own sake: a petrol station shaped as a giant cowboy hat alongside two boots (a girl's to house the ladies' toilets and a guy's to house the gents), and an entire village of wigwams offering a fantasy escape.

The buildings in the second section, 'Wonderwall', catch the eye purely because of the vast murals on their blank exterior walls. Structure cedes entirely to surface treatment, making just as big an impression as complex form. The effect is quite surreal, almost theatrical. It is worth noting that the artist responsible for the murals on Farmer John Meats was a scenic painter for Hollywood films, whose vast vision of an idyllic countryside in the middle of the most built-up industrial area of LA has turned the pig slaughterhouse into a tourist attraction.

The final section, 'Roadside Attractions', focuses on other attention-grabbing methods including typographics, symbols ... and Big Men. The latter tower above roadside stores and warehouses, proudly and comically holding aloft the company's wares or logo. Hardly any of the structures in this chapter are the work of known architects or designers. With a few notable exceptions, most undeniably incline more towards advertising and gimmickry, in many cases with a touch of the Heath Robinsons about them. Most are not architecture in the true sense; but they all provoke a smile, and were an important step along the way to an architecture that doesn't take itself too seriously. *Abigail Grater*

big fun

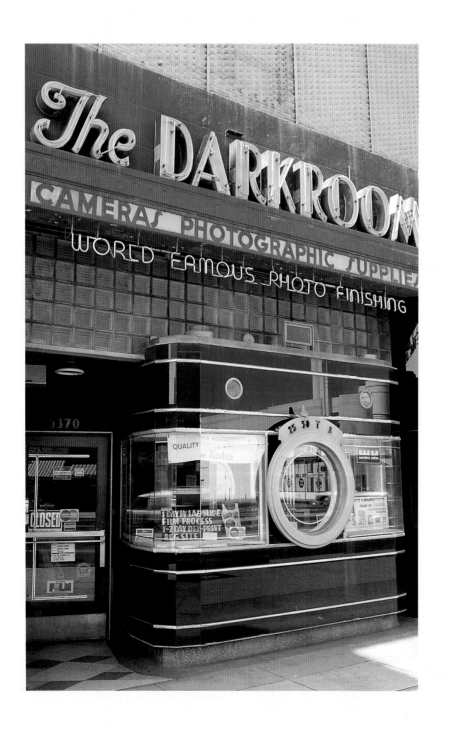

Opposite: Tail o' The Pup, 1946, at the original La Cienega Boulevard location, Los Angeles, California, USA

Left: The Darkroom, Wiltshire Boulevard, Los Angeles, California, USA, 1938 – camera shop in its original state, now a restaurant and unfortunately ruined

North Woods Inn, Los Angeles,
California, USA – winter wonderland

Right: The Tamale, 6421 Whittier Boulevard, Montebello, Los Angeles, California, USA, 1928 – Mexican fast food restaurant still holding on with new use

Below: Burton Factory, Lancashire, England, 1938–9, by Wallis, Gilbert and Partners – cotton bobbin top of Burton Tailoring

Above: The Brown Derby, Wiltshire Boulevard, Los Angeles, California, USA, 1926 (no longer standing)

Left: Orange Juice Stand, Orlando, Florida, USA, 1982

The food of hyperrealism: larger-than-life donuts in Los Angeles, USA

Opposite above: Donut Hole drive-through, La Puente, 1969

Opposite below: Randy's Donuts, La Cienega Boulevard at Manchester Boulevard

Right: Donut King, West Manchester Avenue, Inglewood

Below: Angel Food Donuts

Above: Hat+Boot Texaco Petrol Station, Highway 99, Seattle, Washington, USA (now abandoned) – the boots are the rest rooms!

Right: Good Luck Petrol, Dallas, Texas, USA (now demolished)

Wigwam Village Motel, Foothills
Boulevard, Rialto, California, USA,
1933, by Frank Redford – concrete
comes to canvas

Wigwam Village Motel:
the old Route 66

Capitol Records, 1750 North Vine
Street, Hollywood, California, USA,
1954, by Welton Becket and
Associates – a stack of 45s

Chemosphere' (Malin Residence),
Hollywood, California, USA, 1960, by
John Lautner – close encounters of
the Googie kind

"New York is one of the capitals
of the world and Los Angeles
is a constellation of plastic."

– Norman Mailer, 1969

wonderwall

Right and opposite below:
A&M Records, 1416 North La Brea
Avenue, Hollywood, California,
USA – the old Chaplin film studios

Opposite above: Freeway Lady,
1271 West Temple, Los Angeles,
California, USA, 1974, by Kent
Twitchell – Granny with an MG

Farmer John Meats; 3049 East
Vernon Avenue, Los Angeles,
California, USA, with murals by
Les Grimes – pig slaughterhouse
masquerades as hog heaven

roadside
attractions

Right: Buick car lot, Los Angeles, California, USA, 1960 – refers to 1960s interior design

Opposite: Norms, Santa Monica, Los Angeles, California, USA – Armet & Davis electric pennants on a 1960s coffee shop

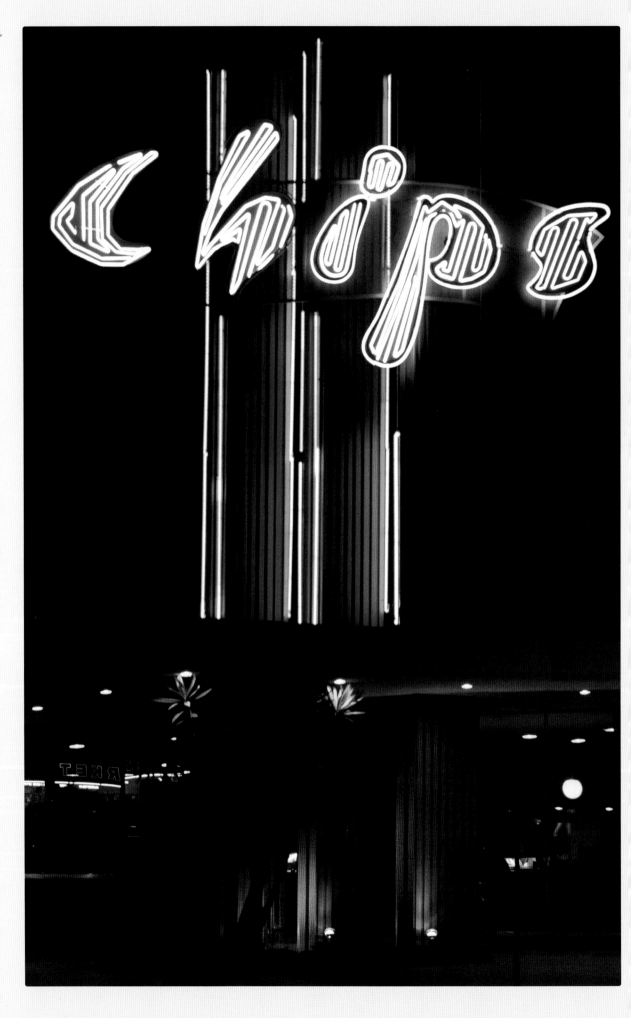

Right: Chips, Los Angeles, California, 1960s – Googie coffee shop using electragraphics to sell at night

Opposite: Chips during the day

"The language of design, architecture and urbanism in Los Angeles is the language of movement."

– Reyner Banham, in *The Architecture of Four Ecologies* (London: Penguin, 1971)

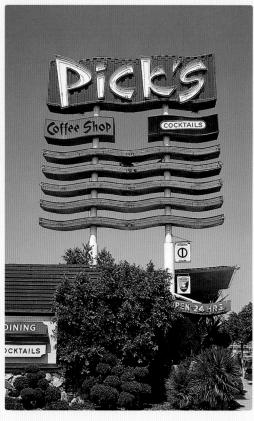

Opposite: The Boys supermarket,
California, USA

Above: Market Basket supermarket –
giant basket weave

Above right: Pick's Coffee Shop,
Los Angeles, California, USA,
1950s – coffee shop with wave sign

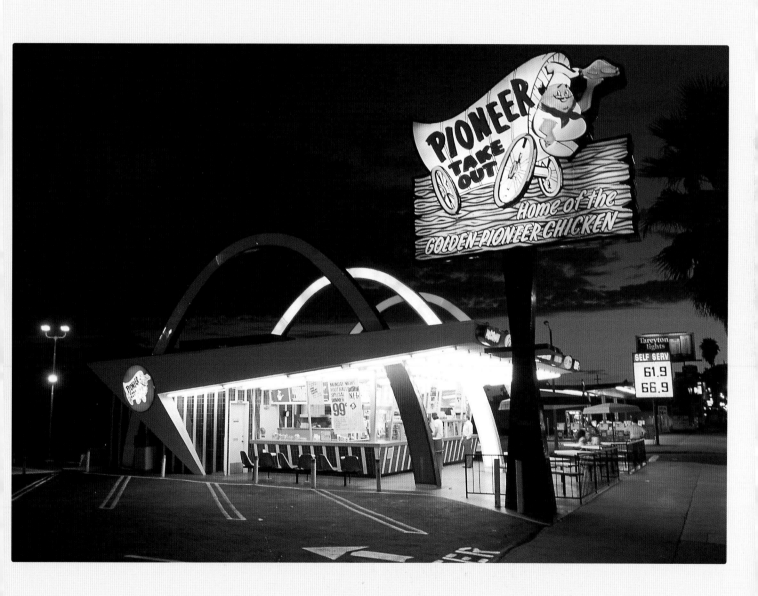

Opposite: Thriftimart supermarket and liquor store, Los Angeles, California, USA – the big T calling all drinkers!

Above: Pioneer Take Out, Hollywood, California, USA at night – the covered wagon come to takeaway

Wonder Bowl Bowling Alley, Los
Angeles, California, USA, early 1960s
– typomatic Big Fun!

Pegs Laundries, Los Angeles,
California, USA, 1960s – giant pegs
with pegged-on graphics

Right: Early McDonalds sign 1959, Downey, California, USA – single 60-ft arch with Speedie, now a defunct symbol

Below: Rockview Milk Farms, Downey, California, USA – cash & carry dairy

Opposite top: Johnie's Coffee Shop, Wiltshire Boulevard, Los Angeles, California, USA – featuring the 'fat boy'

Opposite below: Felix Garage, Figuera Street, Los Angeles, California, USA – Chevrolet car dealership takes on 1920s cartoon character

Below: Johnie's Family Restaurant & Coffee Shop, Firestone Place, Los Angeles, California – typomatic architecture

This page, opposite and overleaf: 'Big Men' in Californian advertising architecture

Above: Carpeteria carpet store

Right: Big Man Tyres – awaiting a new location

Opposite above: Hickory Burger, Pacific Coast Highway, Los Angeles – big man over Malibu

Opposite below: Paint Center, Sacramento – 'scuse me while I paint the sky

Opposite left: Dooley's Garden Shop, Los Angeles, California, USA – giantism like the Village People

Opposite right: Ali Baba Carpet Shop, Hollywood, California, USA – Ali hovering over Hollywood

Below left: Chicken Boy Takeaway, downtown Los Angeles, California, USA – René Magritte-style surrealism

Below right: Circus Liquor, Vineland, Los Angeles, California, USA – electrographic liquor clown

coming
up for air

The buildings shown here represent a great turning point in architecture. After so many years stuck in the white box, there finally came a point when architects had the courage to break free. Virtuous and beautiful as it is when done properly, Modernism lost its monopoly. Suddenly it became accepted that it is possible to produce legitimate architecture that also has an element of wit, or even incorporates references to typographics and advertising.

Among the most successful of architectural quips are SITE's works for the Best Products chain in the USA. Outside opening hours, the Sacramento showroom shown here seems impenetrable save for a small back entrance; but every morning a whole 42-ton corner of the brickwork slides away from the main bulk of the building to invite customers in through the great rupture it leaves. In other stores, a whole wall is lifted up to reveal a hidden glass front underneath, a façade peels off from its corners, or whole sections tumble down into apparent ruin.

The building that caused the greatest stir was Philip Johnson and John Burgee's AT&T Building in New York. Nicknamed the 'Chippendale Highboy' from the start, it is a fairly ordinary office block except for the fact that it sports a huge pediment at its top, and its entrance resembles the spindly legs favoured by the great furniture-makers. This clear though relatively understated visual pun opened the floodgates to ever bolder architectural witticisms.

Perhaps the boldest of all is the Chiat/Day Building with its open reference to the amusing yet unsophisticated roadside advertising architecture of LA and its environs. Unsurprisingly, this extraordinary structure in the form of a pair of binoculars, with conference rooms in its shafts and skylight oculi taking the place of lenses, was built to house the headquarters of an advertising company. It was the result of a unique collaboration between architect (Frank O Gehry) and sculptors (Claes Oldenburg and Coosje van Bruggen).

Other buildings featured have a less clearly defined yet equally potent sense of fun. Gehry's Aerospace Museum features a model aeroplane as a signifier on its main façade, and Michael Graves' Disney hotels sport huge dolphins, swans and related motifs in reference to their names, both recalling the kinds of structures and devices featured in the previous chapter. John Outram's Water Pumping Station in London's Docklands, meanwhile, echoes the Art Deco factories of the second chapter.
Most of these buildings have more complex underlying meanings, whether they be narratives on the anatomy of culture (Outram), comments on the relationship between art and architecture (SITE) or challenges to conventions of architectural form (Eric Owen Moss). At the same time, they are generous buildings which are not lost in the mists of academicism: they can just as easily be enjoyed on a lighter level. *Abigail Grater*

"Please don't give us a flat top."
– AT&T client to Phillip Johnson

"Now that's a building!"
– AT&T Chairman on seeing the model

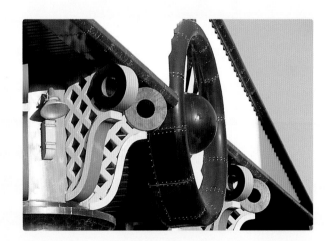

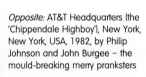

Opposite: AT&T Headquarters (the 'Chippendale Highboy'), New York, New York, USA, 1982, by Philip Johnson and John Burgee – the mould-breaking merry pranksters

Above and right: Water Pumping Station, Docklands, London, England, 1985, by John Outram – cartooning the temple, with Memphis-style columns and mock turbine impeller

Walt Disney World Dolphin Hotel, Epcot Resort Boulevard, Orlando, Florida, USA, 1990, by Michael Graves – Toytown Wedgwood whimsy

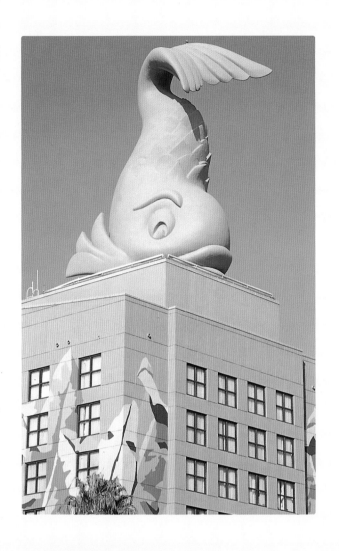

Opposite above: Walt Disney World Dolphin Hotel – giant urn-style fountains

Opposite below left: Walt Disney World Dolphin Hotel – wall painted tropicano

Opposite below right: Walt Disney World Dolphin Hotel – clam shell fountain cascade

Above left: Walt Disney World Dolphin Hotel – dolphin roof symbol, 60ft high

Above right: Walt Disney World Swan Hotel, Epcot Resort Boulevard, Orlando, Florida, USA, 1990, by Michael Graves – swan roof symbol, 60ft high

Left: Walt Disney World Swan Hotel – entrance

99

Best ('The Notch Project'), Arden Fair Shopping Mall, Sacramento, California, USA, 1977, by SITE – architecture seeking publicity

"Magritte-style storefronts."

– Tom Wolf on SITE's work for Best

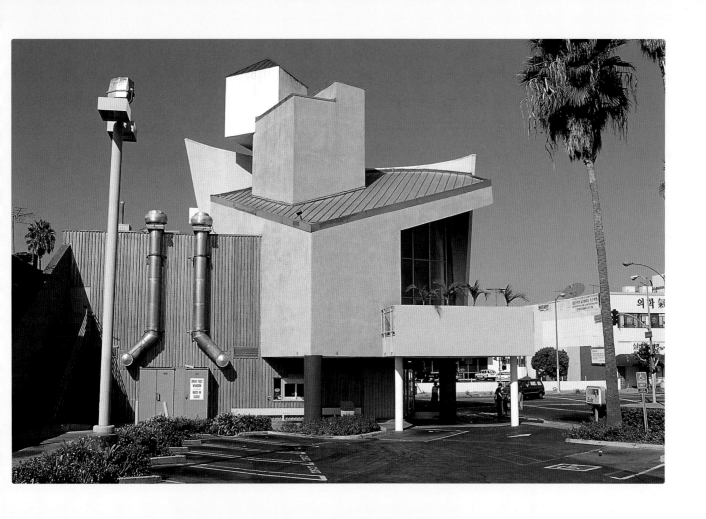

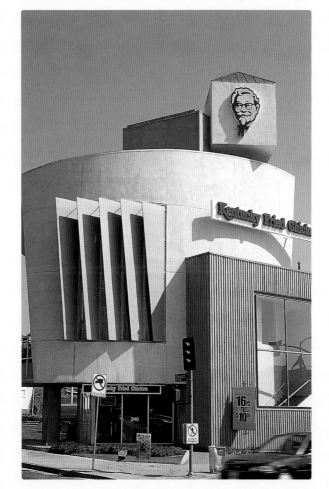

Opposite: Chiat/Day Building, Main Street, Venice Beach, California, USA, 1991, by Frank O Gehry in collaboration with Claes Oldenburg and Coosje van Bruggen – *above:* full view of the sculptured binoculars, continuing the LA tradition of Pop Architecture; *below:* looking up from beneath the binoculars

Above and right: Kentucky Fried Chicken, Hollywood, Los Angeles, California, USA, 1989, by Grinstein/Daniels Architects – the cardboard bucket gets concrete endorsement

Opposite: Kodak Complex, Culver City, California, USA, 1996, by Eric Owen Moss – Teutonic concrete funny face

Below and overleaf: Aerospace Museum, 700 State Drive Exposition Park, Los Angeles, California, USA, 1985, by Frank O Gehry – Frank bolts aeroplanes on the outside and takes roadside attractions into federal architecture

"Palladio faced a fork in the road, and he took the wrong turn. He should have recognised there is chaos."

– Frank O Gehry, quoted by Giles Worsley in The Daily Telegraph, 18 March 2000

the shiny new popularism

In the last five years of the 20th century, buildings began to emerge which were not just inventive in form, but broke all the rules of construction. In these astonishing structures, architects have taken advantage of the latest technologies both to produce the designs of the forms themselves, and to tackle the problem of how to realise those forms successfully on a large scale. These are buildings without precedent.

Frank O Gehry has undoubtedly been the main protagonist in this revolution, and three of his buildings are shown in this section. The earliest – the ice hockey arena he designed for Disney in Anaheim, California – is dominated by a sensuous curving roof which rolls over the vast space like an ocean wave, as if it is about to crash onto the adjacent palm trees.

From this innovative but relatively simple form, Gehry quickly progressed to more outlandish structural feats. The Guggenheim Museum in Bilbao is the most celebrated of these, and caused what must be the greatest flurry of international enthusiasm in the history of architecture. The medium-sized industrial town on the Basque coast of Spain suddenly became one of the most popular European weekend break destinations purely on the basis of this one building, with its extraordinary sensuously curved form clad in glinting titanium. More recently he designed the Seattle Experience Music Project, a museum dedicated to Jimi Hendrix. The forms of this building resemble fragments of guitars, and the vivid colours too are derived from the instruments – specifically those manufactured by Fender in the 1960s.

On a more modest scale, the Lord's Media Centre in London met with universal praise when it opened in 1998. It is one of very few built works by the small London firm Future Systems, which has been turning out dreamy, utopian designs inspired by all manner of forms – natural, mechanical, biological – for some years. It couples ground-breaking structural techniques, using methods usually only employed in boat-building, with an imaginative futuristic shape that has led to it being described as resembling a friendly alien eye. Another new London landmark, Peckham Library combines the bright colours and carefree irregularities of children's drawings with the practicalities of a sustainably designed working library. These two buildings were successive winners of the Stirling Prize, the most noted architectural award in Britain.

Back in the USA, Eric Owen Moss's 'Box' is a commercial office building on top of a reconfigured 1920s warehouse, precariously perched as if it were about to topple. The cantilevering behind this balancing trick is as much of a technical achievement as the bizarre forms of the other buildings featured, and it has an unsettling but playful visual effect. The same architect's nearby 'Umbrella' gives a thrilling twist to an otherwise featureless film production and performance facility, using an explosion of steel and cascading glass.

Perhaps the greatest achievement of these buildings is that they have caused equal excitement in the architectural community and in the public at large. Architecture is something that affects everyone, and yet for many years the gap between the ideals of the profession and the response of the man in the street had been widening. Finally we have reached a point of convergence, where both can celebrate the same structures – the one for their cutting-edge technical achievement, and the other for their sense of character, excitement and fun. *Abigail Grater*

Above, right and opposite: Lord's
Media Centre, Lord's Cricket Ground,
London, UK, 1996, by Future Systems
– boat-building construction meets
the Sony bedside radio

"Lord's spaceship has landed."

– The Times on Lord's Media Centre

Disney Ice, Anaheim, California,
USA, 1995, by Frank O Gehry

Clockwise from above: the swoopy
igloo with the colours of the Mighty
Ducks hockey team; looking like
a metallic moiré mirage; surf's up!

Guggenheim Museum, Bilbao,
Spain, 1997, by Frank O Gehry –
golden fish scales.

Guggenheim Museum, Bilbao

Clockwise from top left: view from
the road bridge, evoking the film-set
expressionism of *The Cabinet of Dr.
Caligari*; lake-side viewing platform;
the Guggenheim art ship docked up
the river Nervion; titanium ship
shapes

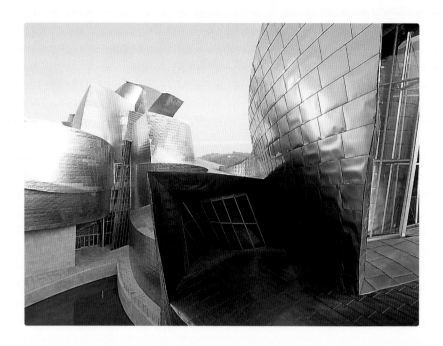

"They wanted a smile"

– Frank O Gehry on the Guggenheim Museum, Bilbao

Opposite top: The Box, Culver City, California, USA, 1994, by Eric Owen Moss – a dropped-on conference room

Opposite bottom: The Umbrella, Culver City, California, USA, 1999, by Eric Owen Moss – office meltdown

Above: Peckham Library, London, England, 2000, by Will Alsop, during the day – back to the future with Dan Dare

Peckham Library – night-time reading

"I see a great splash of cadmium orange across a city."

– Will Alsop

Experience Music Project, Seattle, Washington, USA, 2000, by Frank O Gehry

Right: Monorail emerging from building

Below: Titanium-clad Goods Entrance

Opposite: Orbiter from fairground in front of purple/silver side

"I wanted to evoke the Rock 'n' Roll experience without being too literal about it." – Frank O Gehry on the Seattle Experience Music Project

Experience Music Project, Seattle –
3D architectural experience inspired
by Jimi Hendrix

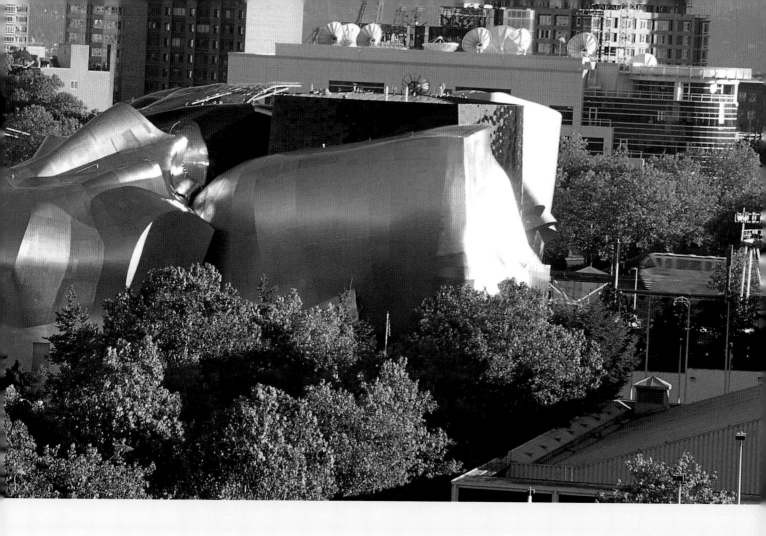

Experience Music Project, Seattle

Opposite: gold side – the monorail enters the building overlooked by the space needle

Above: view from above

Right: gold/red side – roller coaster fretboards

PETER MACKERTICH is a photographer and works from his studio in Camberwell, London. He has been working freelance for 30 years and has many advertising and commercial clients. Previously published work includes *Façade: a decade of British and American commercial architecture* (Matthews Miller Dunbar, London, 1976), featuring 1930s industrial and commercial buildings in London and New York. Blockhaus, an exhibition of his photographs of World War II bunkers curated by the Imperial War Museum, travelled around Europe and North America. For the last ten years, he has taught Design Photography at the London College of Printing.

TONY MACKERTICH spent the early part of his design career creating advertising campaigns for General Motors, COI and Central Television, whilst working for London's leading ad agencies. He co-authored *Façade: a decade of British and American commercial architecture* with his brother Peter. He is currently working as a consultant freelance art director and designer, based in London.

Peter & Tony Mackertich
Invicta Works
8 Graces Mews
London SE5 8JF
petermackertich.com

Above: Peter and Tony behind the 'H' in the Hollywood sign